SUNBURNS TO SNOWSTORMS

UPPER MICHIGAN WEATHER IN PICTURES & STORIES

Karl Bohnak and Jack Deo

SUNBURNS TO SNOWSTORMS

UPPER MICHIGAN WEATHER IN PICTURES & STORIES

Karl Bohnak and Jack Deo

Cover Design: Stacey Willey and Elizabeth Yelland

Edited: Judy Johnson

Interior Layout: Stacey Willey and Elizabeth Yelland

Photographs: Jack Deo

Illustrations: Elizabeth Yelland

Copyright 2017
Cold Sky Publishing, Negaunee, MI
Superior View Studios, Marquette, MI

Print Consultant
Globe Printing, Inc. Ishpeming, MI

Published by Cold Sky Publishing
ISBN 978-0-9778189-1-4

Library of Congress Control Number
2017909088

First Printing July 2017

No portion of this publication may be reproduced, reprinted, or otherwise copied for distribution purposes without express written permission of the authors and publisher.

Acknowledgments

by Karl Bohnak

I would like to thank Marquette Regional History Center Development Director Kaye Hiebel for bringing Jack and me together for a History Center fundraiser presentation. This book grew out of that presentation. Thanks also goes to the Center's Research Librarian, Rosemary Michelin. If you have a question about local history, she does her absolute best to find the answer.

My wife and publishing partner, Liz Yelland, provided the art work for the book along with the general design. I appreciate the visual flair she provided and implicitly trust her artistic eye. Special thanks goes to Stacey Willey. She has developed quite a reputation for book layout and design. Her work made our concept into a tangible reality.

by Jack Deo

This book would have never happened if it wasn't for my high school science teacher Mr. Lee Bartlett. In 10th grade, I took Mr. Bartlett's B&W photography class, where we learned to develop our own film and print our own photographs. The entire classroom could be darkened for printing under safe lights. Mr. Bartlett would count down as he prepared to turn on the lights. I was always the last to put away my photo paper. He would yell, "Deo, you can't beat the light"

That year I bought my first single lens reflective camera, and built my first darkroom. In college I took a color photography course from Mr. Alan Stross. I fell in love with color slide film and always carried both color and black & white film. If you don't think the Arts are important in the schools, think again. It changes lives.

In 1978 I was preparing to open a photography studio in Downtown Marquette. That same year, the photography studio, Childs Art Gallery, closed their doors after 110 years. I obtained many of their negatives, photographs and camera equipment. Thus began a collecting snowball, that led me to obtain many negative and photograph collections throughout the last forty years.

I would like to thank the hundreds of individuals who shared their personal family photographs with me over the last 40 years. Thanks also go to Kaye Hiebel who had the idea to put Karl and me together, and to the Marquette Regional History Center for letting us dive into their photograph collection.

Finally, I want to thank my wife Cindy. None of this would have happened without your constant support. This book is dedicated to you.

Photo Credits

Marquette Regional History Center- Credit, (MRHC):

Both Photos 11	Both Photos 31	Both Photos 102
Bottom Photo. 14	Top Photo 46	Photo 105
Bottom Photo. 16	Top Photo 70	Both Photos 106
Top Photo 21	Photo 100	Photo 138
Both Photos 30	Photo 101	

Negaunee Historical Society
Left Photograph 48

Mary Jayne Hallifax:
Bottom Photo. 29
Both Photos 61

Jim Dwyer:
Photo 37
Top Photos 57
Top Photos 78

Tom Buchkoe:
Photos 39

Helen Micheau:
Photo 40

Brianne Farr:
Photo 47

Delta County Historical Society:
Photo 125
Marion Strahl Boyer:
Photo 126

Jack Deo:
Both Photos 10
Photo 33
Top Photo 34
Bottom Photo. 35
Photo 159

Paula Reynolds:
Special thanks for the photos and information 36
Mike Horton 47

All other photos from the archives of Superior View-superiorview@viewsofthepast.com

Photography takes an instant out of time, altering life by holding it still.
— *Dorothea Lange*

Table of Contents

Acknowledgments 3
Introduction. 6
About the Photos 7
1 Sunburns 9
2 Wildfires 19
3 Floods 27
4 Severe Weather 33
5 Backward Springs 41
6 Snowstorms 49
7 Cleaning Up 63
8 Transportation 79
9 Shipwrecks 97
10 The Greatest Snowstorm 137
11 Winter's Beauty 157
12 Fashion of the Season 167

Introduction

By Karl Bohnak

This book grew out of a fund-raising program for the Marquette Regional History Center. Photo Historian Jack Deo and I presented the program "Sunburns to Snowstorms." Jack combed his extensive collection of historic photos and I coupled them with some of the stories I gleaned of past weather events. Most of them were compiled in my book *"So Cold a Sky."*

It turns out I have stories for a number of events chronicled in Jack's extensive photo collection. The American settlement of the U.P. began not long before photography became a viable option for recording landscapes, portraits and eventually everyday events.

The earliest photo event in this collection goes back to 1868 and the devastating fire that destroyed much of the industrial and business district of Marquette. One of the highlights of the next decade for which Jack has images is the famous "Ice Blockade" of June 1873. Some of the Marquette shipwrecks of the 1880s are covered as well as the firestorm that destroyed the village of Ontonagon in 1896 and then the "Great Snowstorm" of March 1899.

By far most of the photos presented are from the early portion of the 20th century. It starts with what arguably was the worst season for shipwrecks on Lake Superior—the fall of 1905. Then the historic cold spring of 1907 is covered, followed by the great "Washington's Day Blizzard" of 1922, a massive snowstorm in March 1926 as well as a number of photos from the storm against which all others are measured—the "Storm of '38."

There are a number of photos illustrating how Upper Peninsula residents got around back in the old days, especially how they approached the imposing task of snow removal. There are also quaint photos of how folks dressed to stay cool in the summer and warm in the winter.

All photos are from Jack Deo's collection unless otherwise noted.

About the Photos
By Jack Deo

I was into taking weird weather photographs long before I started collecting historic photos. To be a photographer in Michigan's Upper Peninsula, you have to shoot extreme weather. A photo I took of ice in the Chocolay River (below) is typical of my favorites. I called it "U.P.F.O."

When I began collecting old photographs, I always kept my eye out for historic weather images. From snapshots to postcards, our battle against the elements has always been popular to photographers. Frozen lighthouses, flooded streets, snowplows, shipwrecks, are high on my list of collectable images.

Many of the photographs in this book were taken on glass negatives. Some of these were wet plate negatives where liquid chemicals had to be kept from freezing. Some of the photographers were amateur and some were professional. The images in this book came from my 40 years of collecting.

Some of the photographers who are responsible for images in this book are Samual Bailey, Christian Brubaker, Edward Butler, Thomas Bennet, B.F. Childs, Charles Cole, Ard Emery, William Hook, J.W. Nara, Gustav Werner, Andrew Young, Henry Robb, and Ike Wood.

What history tells us is that some things remain the same; particularly the weather—it's always changing! This is especially true in Upper Michigan. The changeable weather is a reliable source of conversation, occasional frustration and sometimes amazement. We feel the photographs that follow prove this point.

Taking an image, freezing a moment, reveals how rich reality truly is.
— *Anonymous*

Sunburns to Snowstorms: Upper Michigan Weather in Pictures & Stories

This was the trendy fashion in swimwear early in the 20th century. Pictured are Blanche Harrison and friends in Champion Michigan circa 1915.

1

Sunburns

Summer is usually a comfortable time of year in Upper Michigan. Average high temperatures range from the mid-70s along the Great Lakes shores to around 80 over interior sections near the Wisconsin line. Nighttime lows average in the mid-50s to near 60.

There are occasional episodes of hot weather. An average summer will produce three days with 90 degrees or above at the National Weather Service (NWS) near Negaunee. Southern locations like Iron Mountain average a couple more. Streaks of consecutive days of 90 degrees or above are rare, so when one occurs, it lingers in the memories of U.P. residents. This was likely especially true in the old days before air conditioning. However even today not all residents have the luxury of air conditioning because it's used so seldom and some prefer to tough it out and just endure the few uncomfortable days.

While temperatures in the 90s are infrequent, readings at or above 100 degrees are exceedingly rare. For instance in Iron Mountain, Upper Michigan's warmest city in the summer, the last time it hit 100 degrees was on July 16, 2006. The previous 100-degree day was June 18, 1995 and prior to that July 26, 1955—forty years earlier!

"The thing with heat is, no matter how cold you are, no matter how much you need warmth, it always, eventually, becomes too much."—Victoria Aveyard

The contrast between seasons, particularly winter and summer, is stark and extreme. For instance in the dead of winter, it is difficult to wrap one's mind around the fact that a frozen, desolate shoreline will become a beautiful white sand beach perfect for sunbathing in just a few short months.

Chapter • 1 • Sunburns

Above, sunbathing ladies on Black Rocks at Presque Isle in Marquette circa 1900. Below, swimmers cool off about the turn of the 20th century; a time that featured the hottest day on record in Upper Michigan.

On July 15, 1901 the official U.S. Weather Bureau thermometer in Marquette topped out at 108 degrees. The young men and women pictured here probably spent most of their time that day in the chilly water of Lake Superior. Those who stayed in town boarded the open-air street cars in an attempt to catch a cooling breeze.

Chapter • 1 • Sunburns

It was so hot a U.S. Weather Bureau observer stated "Marquette had better take down her shingle as the Queen Summer Resort of the North"

Sunburns to Snowstorms: Upper Michigan Weather in Pictures & Stories

Above, a favorite swimming hole in the Gwinn area. This was the place to be for area children to cool off. Below, a group photo taken at Black Rocks, Presque Isle. The man pictured in the photo below exhibited the usual protocol of a Victorian man during the summer; a long-sleeve shirt and tie with a wool blazer and trousers. During the heat wave of 1901 new fashion ground was broken as men were "emboldened to cast their coats aside." They walked the streets in shirt sleeves and some did away with suspenders altogether!

Chapter • 1 • Sunburns

Top photo taken at Houghton circa 1890. Middle and bottom photos from Bass Lake in Gwinn just before the turn of the 20th century. A local merchant advertised "Hot Weather Fixings" in a local newspaper during the first decade of the 20th century. It exhorted the potential male customer to "be comfortable this hot weather…(with)…A Suit of Bon Bon Underwear." It was probably so hot the day these photos were taken that these young men did away with underwear altogether.

The hottest week in recorded history occurred during the hottest decade—the sizzling 1930s. In these days before air conditioning, area residents sought relief by sleeping in the open air. Above, the canvas tents in this photo would have been too hot to sleep in after a day with a high temperature around 100 degrees. The Marketty boys of Gwinn, posing in this photo at Bass Lake, would have probably slept under the stars. Below, there was also some hot steamy weather in the 1950s, particularly the summer of 1955. These sunbathers were photographed about that time at Presque Isle in Marquette.

Chapter • 1 • Sunburns

The week of July 7-13, 1936 Iron Mountain reached 100 degrees or above on six of the seven days and 99 the other day. In Munising the temperature peaked above 100 degrees for seven consecutive hours on July 13.

These bathing beauties would have probably emerged from the water only briefly for the camera. It was so hot, sailors on a freighter 10 miles off shore from Marquette reported a temperature over 100 degrees on one of the days.

The heat lingered into the 1940s particularly August 1947. A convertible would have provided some relief when the temperature in Houghton soared to 103 degrees on August 5, 1947. The mean temperature in Marquette for the month was 70.9 degrees; over seven degrees above average.

The warmest decade in Upper Michigan was the 1940s. At Ironwood where consistent records were kept since the beginning of the 20th century the mean annual temperature never dropped below 40 degrees. Even in the first decade of the 21st century, touted by some as the warmest on record, four of 10 years had a mean annual temperature below 40 degrees.

2

Wildfires

In a normal year the Upper Peninsula receives enough precipitation distributed evenly through the seasons so that the wildfire danger is kept in check. The worst potential time for fires is in the spring before green up just after the snow melts. A secondary season can occur after an exceptionally hot, dry summer.

Fires devastated Upper Michigan during and just after the lumbering boom of the late 19th and early 20th centuries. At that time poor forestry practices set the stage for disaster. A company would cut tracts of virgin timber indiscriminately and leave the slash behind to dry. This cut-over or "wasteland" would become fuel for devastating fires. The most famous was the Peshtigo Fire of October 1871. This fire originated near Peshtigo in northeastern Wisconsin and jumped the Menominee River into Michigan. It wiped out the village of Birch Creek north of Menominee in Upper Michigan. Other widespread fires occurred regularly in spring and sometimes late summer and fall well into the first and second decades of the 20th century. Gradually forest practices focusing on prevention and land stewardship resulted in less fires consuming less acreage.

While wildfires are generally less widespread and destructive than a century ago, they still are a threat when conditions are right. The most recent example was the Duck Lake fire north of Newberry that began in late May 2012. The fire was set off by lightning and burned out of control for several days. By the time the fire was fully contained in mid-June it had burned over 21, 000 acres with the loss of 136 structures including 49 cabins and homes including a motel and store.

"If the forest has a day of fire and the heat of the flames does not consume a special tree, it will still be changed; charred, but still standing."—Dan Groat

The earliest photograph of an Upper Michigan fire was taken after the frontier village of Marquette was laid to waste by flames in June 1868. The fire was not specifically weather related. However wind did fan the flames and helped to make the destruction of the downtown area complete. Below is another image of the aftermath of the fire directed toward the lake. Interestingly, the fire actually started in the dock area on the left and then spread uptown.

At that time, nearly all the buildings in the downtown were made of wood. After the fire, the city fathers passed a law banning wood structures in the business district. Below, another view of the growing community of Marquette circa mid-to-late 19th century.

Ontonagon was a thriving village in the latter days of the 19th century. Diamond Match Company set up their headquarters in town and took advantage of the abundant pine trees nearby. Logs were driven down the Ontonagon River and then processed into matchsticks, shingles and boxes at two huge company sawmills near the river's mouth.

Chapter • 2 • Wildfires

The town boasted a fully staffed fire department with a horse-drawn fire-wagon, while (below) lumber camps outside of town were working at full capacity. Logs were driven down the Ontonagon River and then processed into matchsticks, shingles and boxes. In late August 1896 piles of lumber were said to be stacked three stories high at the Diamond Match Plant. Nearby were enormous piles of sawdust. The Diamond Match Company was an enormous pile of kindling ready to burst into flames.

Del Woodbury was 17 years old on August 25, 1896. Here he is being interviewed by outdoor TV show host Mort Neff in the 1960s.

On that August day he remembers "the sun was just a red ball up there... we had been bothered by smoke for, oh, a number of days." This day was particularly warm and dry. The wind picked up until about 1:00 in the afternoon the lighthouse keeper reported it was "hot and blowing a living gale."

The swamp southeast of the light caught fire and the wind spread it toward Diamond Match. Firefighters and plant workers tried to beat back the flames, but to no avail. The towering stacks of lumber caught fire and the devastation began. When the fire jumped the river and reached the piles of sawdust, the town itself was doomed.

Diamond Match along with much of the village of Ontonagon was laid to waste in a matter of a few hours. A total of 344 buildings burned to the ground including 300 homes. In one afternoon 2,000 residents became homeless. The bodies of charred cows, pigs, poultry, dogs and cats were strewn about the burn area which encompassed a full square mile.

A number of victims spent the first night sleeping in the open air with their only possessions the clothes on their backs. Soon the state militia arrived and put up 150 tents at the fair grounds. The refugee camp became known as White City and housed up to several hundred people well into the fall. The Village of Ontonagon gradually rose from the ashes of that terrible August day. The resiliency of the town folk is exemplified by Banker C. Meilleur who set up a make-shift structure to conduct business a mere 48 hours after the fire.

3

Floods

Spring is usually the time of year that the worst, most extensive flooding occurs in Upper Michigan. The flooding results from snow melt accompanied by heavy rain. This type of flooding occurs at least to a minor extent during most springs; major snow melt floods are relatively rare.

The record floods of recent times have several factors in common: a deep snow pack, heavy rain and an extreme spike in temperature. This combination occurred in April 1985. Heavy rain fell on a thick, waterlogged snow cover and then an early summer heat wave pushed temperatures up over 80 degrees. The resulting flood was labeled a 100-year event. Then, 17 years later, almost the exact scenario repeated itself. After the record snow season of 2001-02 (319.8 inches recorded at the National Weather Service near Negaunee, compared to an average of around 200 inches), a heavy rain event at mid-month was followed by a stretch of summer weather with highs in the 70s and 80s. Serious flooding followed with the worst conditions in the western and central Upper Peninsula. Wakefield's Sunday Lake nearly inundated the town, and a desperate community effort kept the city substation—the main power supply into the community—from flooding.

Occasionally, summer rains will lead to flooding. The most recent examples of this was the July flood of 2016 in far western Upper Michigan. A continuous line of thunderstorms moving over the same area the evening of July 11 dropped up to a foot of rain in far western Gogebic and Ontonagon Counties washing out roads and bridges. Later that year in the fall, torrential rains washed out roads and bridges in a small portion of Marquette County.

Looking back even further, history shows far western Upper Michigan is especially vulnerable to summer floods. In July 1909, a daily-record rain of 6.72 inches in Ironwood on July 21 was followed the next day by five inches of rain. Serious summer flooding also struck the western U.P. in 1942 and 1946. The 1940s had another extreme event when Marquette and vicinity was flooded with over five inches of rain in one day during late July 1949.

"The great floodgates of the wonder-world swung open."—Herman Melville

Ontonagon has not only been damaged by fire but by water, too. Unseasonably warm weather and thick, solid ice left from one of the coldest winters of the 20th century resulted in record flooding on the Ontonagon River in early April 1963. Heavy runoff met with solid ice near the mouth of the river and caused heavy flooding in the village. River street lived up to its name and became navigable by boat at the height of the flood. Some businesses in town were soaked with icy water up to four feet deep. When the water receded, a thick coat of red silt mixed in places with oily substances, covered everything that came in contact with the water. Truckloads of food-stuffs and other merchandise ended up in the village dump. Conservative estimates placed damage at over a half-million dollars.

Chapter • 3 • Floods

Above, due to its geography and location, Escanaba is prone to flash flooding even today. This circa 1920s photo illustrates an example of that flooding.

Many U.P. cities are prone to occasional flash flooding during summer thunderstorms. For instance, Marquette and vicinity was battered with torrential rains on July 28, 1949. Damage was principally to buildings, roads and railroad right-of-ways. The month brought 10.20 inches of rain to Marquette, the wettest July on record.

Below, is an example of flash flooding in Munising circa 1950s.

Above was the scene at Marquette City Dam #2 on the Dead River in June 1939. Not only was there high water due to heavy rain, but on June 16, 1939 a tremendous "tidal wave" or seiche occurred on the Lake Superior basin in conjunction with severe weather that tore across Upper Michigan.

The Dead River below with the surge of water off Lake Superior pushing the river upstream. A seiche is a rhythmic oscillation of a body of water. Seiches on Lake Superior occur when prolonged strong winds push water toward one side of the lake causing water levels to rise on the downwind side of the lake and to drop on the windward side. When the wind stops, the water sloshes back and forth.

Above, the Dead River during low tide of the seiche; and below, during high tide. The seiche pushed and pulled the water of Lake Superior in and out of Marquette Bay at half-hour intervals. The freakish surge "unprecedented in the memory of marine men" rose and fell five feet for several hours. Docks, fish houses and small boats sustained extensive damage on June 16, 1939.

These men pictured near Rapid River in about 1915 were working on a flood damaged railroad bed. Extensive flooding below was probably caused by spring snow melt.

Precipitation Extremes for Upper Michigan

Wettest Month: 15.45", July 1909, Ironwood

Driest Month: 0.00", January 1969, Manistique

Largest Rainstorm: 11.72" July 21-22, 1909, Ironwood

Wettest Day: 6.72" July 21, 1909, Ironwood

Wettest Day Sault Ste. Marie: 5.92", August 3, 1974

Wettest Day Marquette: 5.16", July 20, 1878

Wettest Day Iron Mountain: 4.06", August 29, 1941

Wettest Day Houghton: 3.58", May 17, 1896 & Sep. 4, 2007

Wettest Day Munising: 3.51", May 31, 1970

Wettest Day NWS: 4.29", September 4, 2007

4
Severe Weather

While far from Tornado Alley, Upper Michigan receives its fair share of summer thunderstorms. Occasionally these storms produce dangerous lightning, damaging winds, hail and rarely tornadoes.

"It is only in sorrow, bad weather masters us; in joy we face the storm and defy it." —Amelia Barr

Above, lightning strokes at Presque Isle, Marquette captured by Jack Deo circa 1970s. Bottom is a much earlier photograph of lightning, taken at Marquette Harbor.

Lightning did extensive damage to residences in the late 19th and early 20th centuries. This may be due in part to the fact that buildings were the highest objects in the area after the forests of Upper Michigan had been clear cut. For instance, on the afternoon of June 19, 1878 a lightning bolt entered an Ishpeming home through the chimney; it toppled a stove containing a fire and knocked down a woman standing near the stove. Her shoes and stockings were ripped from her feet while her clothes were "rent and torn." She received serious injuries; her face and limbs were blackened and lacerated. She did survive but likely had a fear of the lightning produced by thunderstorms the rest of her life.

Chapter • 4 • Severe Weather

Above, a lightning bolt strikes Lake Superior off Marquette Harbor. Below, hailstorms most frequently strike Upper Michigan in early summer when the air aloft is still cold. The intense hailstorm of June 20, 2007 in Marquette damaged homes and countless automobiles with hailstones up to three inches in diameter.

It was a dreary spring day on May 10, 1911. Children at Washington school in the Dickinson County community of Felch were outside during recess when a thunderstorm struck. A brother and sister, Carl and Minnie Dixon each ran into different doors of the school.

Both were struck by a bolt of lightning. Minnie was knocked unconscious but survived. Her brother, Carl (pictured below) had steel marbles in his pocket which evidently acted as a conductor to the electricity. He was killed instantly. The school caught fire and efforts to save it were in vain. It burned to the ground.

Chapter • 4 • Severe Weather

Lightning killed 12 horses huddled together during a storm in the Newberry area on August 19, 1904. A man working in a barn some distance away felt a slight shock and 2 other workers in the nearby bush had their axes torn out of their hands. Note the large structure on the horizon. It stands out as the only object in a bleak landscape devoid of trees; a result of the practice of clear cutting at the turn of the 20th century.

Extensive damage to a farm at Bumbletown north of Calumet in Keweenaw County at the turn of the century. The damage was said to be the result of a tornado. Below is a view of the village again against a landscape completely devoid of trees.

On August 16, 1988 an intense squall-line developed over Lake Superior just northwest of Marquette and blasted through the city during the mid-morning. Winds estimated at up to 90 miles per hour blew down hundreds of trees on Presque Isle and throughout the surrounding area. Below, a sign was damaged at an area business to the east of the city.

The Gladstone tornado of July 19, 1992 looked like a well developed Plains tornado as it headed toward the city.

Tornadoes of F-2 intensity or greater and/or tornadoes that have injured or killed since 1950:

May 6, 1984 Alger Co. F-2 Deaths: 0 Injuries: 0
Aug. 22, 1968 Baraga Co. F-2 Deaths: 0 Injuries: 0
July 20, 1972 Delta Co. F-2 Deaths: 0 Injuries: 1
Sept. 16, 1972 Menominee Co. F-2 Deaths: 0 Injuries: 0
Aug. 15, 1978: Iron Co. F-1 Deaths: 0 Injuries: 1
June 14, 1981: Iron Co. F-2 Deaths: 0 Injuries: 0
July 14, 1984: Schoolcraft Co. F-2 Deaths: 0 Injuries: 2
June 8, 1985: Menoninee Co. F-1 Deaths: 1 Injuries: 0
July 4, 1986: Menoninee Co. F-3 Deaths: 0 Injuries: 12
July 11, 1987 Dickinson Co. F-3 Deaths: 0 Injuries: 0
May 11, 1991 Menominee Co. F-3 Deaths: 0 Injuries: 0
July 19, 1992: Delta Co. F-2 Deaths: 0 Injuries: 2
July 5, 1993 Mackinac Co. F-1 Deaths: 0 Injuries: 1

(Data courtesy of The Tornado Project: www.tornadoproject.com)

5

Backward Springs

Spring is a trying time for many Upper Peninsula residents. After a long winter the atmosphere warms only slowly while the waters of the Great Lakes warm even slower. At times the slog toward spring is interrupted by a snowstorm. In some years, there is little or no spring at all but a disagreeable, muddled "winter-spring" season in which a snow cover stays on the ground well past the astronomical date that signals the vernal equinox.

To be fair, the record provides evidence of warm early springs. For instance, the winter of 1877-78 was the warmest on record. Male residents of Marquette walked the streets in shirt sleeves and summer straw hats on Valentine's Day. The unseasonable warmth then continued into early spring. The sounds of "peepers" or swamp frogs were heard in the region before St. Patrick's Day. Farmers around Ishpeming and Negaunee were readying their fields for planting before the first day of astronomical spring. More recently Upper Michigan basked in early summer weather during March 2012. For five consecutive days high temperatures rose into the mid-70s to around 80 degrees. The month as a whole came in at over 15 degrees above average. The mean temperature of 39.7 degrees was nearly a degree warmer than the following April which was still over a degree above average!

On the other hand early summer warmth can be just an unseasonable tease. Temperatures soared into the mid-80s to near 90 on three consecutive late April days in 1990. A couple of weeks later a record May snowstorm blasted the U.P. with nearly two feet of snow at some locations!

"Every year they kill a lot of poets for writing about 'Beautiful Spring.'"—Mark Twain

The famous "Ice Blockade" of 1873 was beautifully recorded by early U.P. photographer B.F. Childs. It is hard to believe that these pictures were taken in June of that year. A number of winters during the 1870s to 1880s were harsh (with the stark exception of 1877-78). A barometer showing how harsh was the arrival of the first boat in Marquette Harbor. In the days before icebreakers, ships were completely at the mercy of weather and ice conditions. The latest arrival on record was May 20, 1875.

Chapter • 5 • Backward Springs

Above, another view of the Ice Blockade. Below, these "Prisoners" were stuck in the ice on April 21-22, possibly sometime in the 1910s.

Upper Michigan residents endured the most backward spring in 1907. A major snowstorm hit much of the U.P. on April 7. Above is a scene from Houghton during this snowy fourth month. Trains were blocked around this city for the first time all winter. Another storm "resumed hostilities" on the 11th and still another brought more snow at mid-month. Below, Calumet looked like mid-winter during the "spring" month of April 1907.

Chapter • 5 • Backward Springs

An old Copper Country resident stated late in the month "I have been here since 1851 and I have never seen anything like this." At month's end, 200 vessels were reported trapped in ice off Whitefish Point. The first boat of the season did not arrive in Marquette until April 27; the latest arrival in years.

May continued the disagreeably cold weather. Snow fell across much of Upper Michigan on May 27, 1907. "It melted rapidly," wrote a Copper Country reporter because "the language used when the 'beautiful' started to fall was sufficiently warm to melt more than snow." The photo below shows the dusting of snow at Ludington Park in Escanaba. What is most remarkable is the absence of leaf growth on the tree in the foreground even though it was May 27!

Chapter • 5 • Backward Springs

History repeats itself! Above on June 1, 1996 Brianne Farr poses at the ice-clogged Lower Harbor in Marquette. Below, eighteen years later, she proudly displays the same date at a position a little farther east in the harbor area. The spring of 1996 was one of the most backward in history featuring heavy late-season snow after a long, snowy winter. The winter of 2013-14 was one of the most consistently cold seasons in the record books and the chill extended through the spring.

Left, a snowman in Negaunee proudly displays his birth date. Up to six inches of snow accumulated June 2-3, 1945 in the Negaunee-Ishpeming area. Right, selling a surplus supply of snow in Ishpeming circa 1990s.

U.P. Winter Weather Extremes

Coldest: -49, Humboldt, Marquette County, February 10, 1899

Coldest month: -7.2, Watersmeet January 1912

Coldest winter: 5.1, Crystal Falls and Bergland, 1978-79

Warmest winter: 30.9, Marquette, 1877-78

"The first day of spring is one thing and the first spring day is another. The difference between them is sometimes as great as a month." —Henry Van Dyke

6

Snowstorms

One of Upper Michigan's distinguishing features is heavy snow. It is the snowiest non-mountainous region east of the Rockies. Snow falls frequently in the Lake Superior snow belts of the northern U.P. In fact when the wind is right, a snowstorm can rage for days in portions of the western U.P. up into the Copper Country and also in the east-central U.P. around Munising.

The big U.P.-wide "synoptic" snowstorms are less frequent but have the greatest impact. These storms do not occur in every winter. Some occur very early or late with no noteworthy events through the majority of the winter season. Good examples of the former include the big snowstorm of November 10-11, 2014. It brought over three feet of snow to portions of the western U.P. and greatly hampered the deer hunting season later in the month. Another is the infamous storm of May 9-10, 1990. After record-breaking heat in late April, a winter storm brought nearly two feet of wet, heavy snow to the central U.P. with around a foot common throughout western sections.

Some of the great snowstorms are remembered for years after. The most notorious are the out of season storms or the ones that affect travel during a holiday.

Downtown Newberry, 1910

"Blow high, blow low, not all its snow could quench our hearth's-fire ruddy glow."
—*John Greenleaf Whittier*

This was the scene in Ishpeming presumably after the "great snowstorm" in mid-March 1899. It followed an Arctic Attack that plunged the temperature as low as 40 below zero in Upper Michigan and brought misery and inconvenience to a vast portion of the nation. At the peak of the cold wave, ice floes appeared at the mouth of the Mississippi River in New Orleans; a phenomenon observed only once before in 1784. Below, The aftermath of another March storm in the Copper Country 14 years later

Chapter • 6 • Snowstorms

One of the more outstanding winter storms to strike the entire Upper Peninsula began just before Washington's birthday, February 21, 1922. The storm raged for the next two days. Even Menominee in the far southern U.P. received an estimated two feet of snow with drifts up to 10 feet deep. Disruptions in communication and travel were reported all the way north to the Copper Country, west to Ironwood and east to the Sault. Below, these young people took a breather from skiing to pose and give us a perspective of how high the snow banks were after the February 1922 storm.

The same youngsters from the previous page take time to record a memory of a beautiful sunny day in the snow. The month of February 1922 brought over two-and-a-half feet of snow to Marquette, most of it falling in this one memorable storm.

Chapter • 6 • Snowstorms

Some landmarks on these Ishpeming City streets can still be seen today.

Above, a plow struggles down Iron Street in Negaunee after a snowstorm in early March 1926. The winter of 1925-26 started quickly with a significant storm in mid-October. However the rest of the winter had only light snow until this one hit. Below, snow drifted streets and sidewalks of Hancock in the wake of the storm.

Chapter • 6 • Snowstorms

The Copper Country in the aftermath of a very snowy period. Below, even without a major snowstorm frequent lake effect snow and cold temperatures pile the snow high and deep in much of the northern U.P. This is a scene in Ishpeming.

A boy shows us how tall the snowbanks were in Calumet. Bottom, finally a sunny day with no snow falling along a snow covered roadway.

Chapter • 6 • Snowstorms

Piled high and deep! The top two images are from the Newberry area. Left, a telephone line worker shows how deep the snow is along the side of the road during the early 1930s. Right, these children show that the snow is even deeper in this 1960s image. Bottom, two vehicles in Marquette were buried by the "Wild March Blizzard" of March 5-6, 1959. It was considered the worst storm in 20 years.

During the height of the early March 1959 storm most highways became impassable. Cars were stranded everywhere including on major state and federal roads. In Delta County, a plow driver clearing a rural road nearly three days after the storm discovered a couple waiting to be rescued. They became stranded the night the storm began.

Chapter • 6 • Snowstorms

A foot or more of wind-whipped snow fell over most of the Upper Peninsula. The U.S. Weather Bureau in Marquette measured a total of 13.6 inches during the March 5-6, 1959 storm.

It was a wide-ranging storm that covered the entire Upper Peninsula bringing travel to nearly a standstill in most locations. Below, in Munising a "lifeline" was set up to guide workers into the paper mill. They followed a rope into the mill and the next day their cars were gone—buried in the deep, drifted snow.

Surprise! Workers clear snow from around the window of an area hospital. Below, In the city, 45 students at Washington Elementary school were forced to spend the night in their classrooms after their bus "became hopelessly stuck."

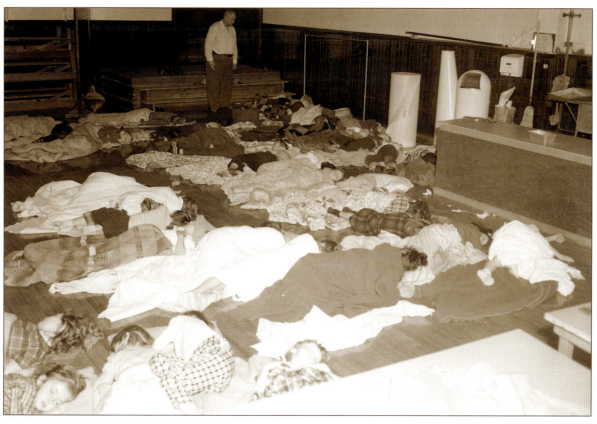

Downtown Sault Ste. Marie after the historic snowstorm of December 8-10, 1995.

Upper Michigan Snowfall Extremes

Biggest snowstorm: 61.7 inches, Sault Ste. Marie, December 8-10, 1995

Snowiest Day (24 hour calendar day): 29 inches, Ishpeming, October 23, 1929

Snowiest month: 133.7 inches, Delaware, December 2000

Deepest snowcover: 63 inches, NWS office near Negaunee, March 14, 1997

Snowiest winter: 390.4 inches, Delaware, 1978-79

Least snowiest winter: 15.8 inches, Escanaba, 1899-1900

"In seed time learn, in harvest teach, in winter enjoy."—William Blake

7

Cleaning Up

Upper Michigan is the snowiest non-mountainous area east of the Rockies. Clearing and disposing of the huge amounts of snow is a way of life and this endeavor has always been a challenge. Back in the old days, crews of men were employed to shovel stretches of roadway. Horses pulled snow rollers across city streets to compress the snow and when the spring thaw came, there must have been a load of impassable slush.

As the 20th century wore on, more and more of the snow clearing was done with plows powered by trucks and tractors. These vehicles were much less powerful than today's counterparts and in a big storm, they'd get bogged down. For instance, after the Storm of '38, it took up to a week to open up all the roads in Marquette County. Back then 19 snow plows and tractors were responsible for clearing 742 miles of roads in the county. Six decades later the amount of equipment doubled (and became more powerful and efficient) while the amount of roadway only increased by 70 percent. The major thoroughfares are well taken care of by today's County Highway Commissions.

"There is no such thing as bad weather, only soft people."—Bill Bowerman

Before the days of snowplows, a crew took a break from shoveling to pose for a photo opportunity on a Calumet street. Below, another Calumet scene. These men and horses had a big job ahead of them.

Chapter • 7 • Cleaning Up

The image above shows just how deep the snow got on a Calumet street circa 1900. The snow got compressed rather than removed. The spring thaw must have been a sloppy, impassable mess. Below a horse-drawn wagon in Houghton circa 1900 removes another load of snow.

Above, an interesting perspective showing work horses in action while below, a street in Munising is already sporting huge snow banks on January 10, 1911. Today U.P. villages and city crews haul away snow. Back in the early 20th century, the snow banks grew and grew all winter.

Chapter • 7 • Cleaning Up

Above, hand shoveling Sixth Street in Calumet circa 1900. Below, 10 horses were either being led to or from a shift hauling away snow in the Copper Country.

Some gentlemen enjoying a nice day after a snowstorm. This was probably taken in March judging by the melt water on the sidewalk. Below a crew works down a street sporting some early model automobiles.

Chapter • 7 • Cleaning Up

Above and below, both showing examples of the horse-drawn Snow Roller; a device used to compress snow to facilitate easy travel by sleigh.

Above is a close-up of a wooden snow roller, courtesy of the J.M. Longyear Research Library. Below is a Steel-plated, 2-drum snow roller once used to "pank" (unique Upper Peninsula verb meaning to compress snow) snow on the roads of Keweenaw County. This roller was donated by Calumet Township to the Eagle River Lighthouse Museum, where you can still see it on display today.

Do you wonder what that man is doing on the right next to the snow roller? He's sitting on it! Winter employment must have been near 100 percent back in the old days. They even employed workers to add weight to help compress the snow.

Republic in southwestern Marquette County was once a thriving mining community. Pictured here is a fleet of tractors ready to do battle with the snowdrifts. Below, a road crew proudly poses with an early, immense version of the wing plow.

Chapter • 7 • Cleaning Up

Above, this tractor seemed to be no match for this snow-clogged road. Below, a rotary plow widens a road near Newberry probably in the late 1940s or early 50s.

Above, a wing plow cuts a path through a U.P. road. Today's plows throw the snow some distance from the highway. These early plows piled the snow right up against the roadway creating huge snowbanks. Below, the plows got bigger and more powerful as the 20th century unfolded.

Chapter • 7 • Cleaning Up

These two photographs are examples of "Snow-gos." In the mid-20th century powerful snow blowers were built onto tractors. These blowers ushered in the modern era of snow removal. The "Snow-gos" loaded snow onto trucks to haul away from city streets.

Above, M-28 near Munising probably in the 1920s. Notice how the road, a major state thoroughfare, is reduced to nearly one lane. Below, this young lady is probably stuck in the slushy snow on an Alger County highway after an unspecified March snowstorm.

Chapter • 7 • Cleaning Up

Pictured next to an enormous rotary plow is Caesar Lucchesi. He ran a bus company in the Copper Country during the early 20th century. Dissatisfied with snow removal on the roads, Lucchesi traveled nearly 400 miles to purchase this plow he saw on a visit to St. Paul, Minnesota. The enterprising businessman made sure the roads were clear and his buses kept rolling. Below, a Calumet "Snow-go" creates an immense cloud of snow as it clears a road after a snowstorm.

Above right, Sault Ste. Marie buried in deep snow; left, more deep snow in Newberry, January 1911. Below, the U.P. snow belts are a place where strong backs are needed. This tried and true method of snow removal is still practiced today by a number of U.P. residents.

"Many 'Human' beings say that they enjoy the winter, but what they really enjoy is feeling proof against it." —Richard Adams

8

Transportation

During Upper Michigan's pioneer days, the main mode of transportation was by boat to and from villages which grew near the shores of mainly Lake Superior. The interior of the peninsula was thick wilderness with only a few trails. Travel was almost easier in the winter when snowshoes were employed. Early pioneer John Forster wrote, "In the absence of beaten roads or trails, snowshoeing was the only mode of locomotion in that new country. The thick underbrush and all fallen timber were buried under the snow, so that in a level country, a smooth, clean park-like plain lay before you."

Settlements eventually grew and by the latter portion of 19th century, railroads opened up the interior U.P. wilderness to travel. Eventually roads were built that facilitated transportation by wheel in the warm season and runners in the winter. In the cities, electrification made trolley traffic possible.

Weather has always had an impact on transportation. Winter was (and still is) the most challenging season for Upper Peninsula wayfarers. On the following pages, you'll see how residents have succeeded (and failed!) in overcoming these winter weather obstacles.

"[About the weather]...there is is only one thing certain about it; you are certain there is going to be plenty of it."—Mark Twain

Above, an open-air "stagecoach" filled to capacity in Newberry. Outside of snowshoes, horse-drawn sleighs were the main mode of overland travel until the railroads were developed into the Upper Michigan interior late in the 19th century. Below, another stagecoach sleigh; this photo was taken in Alger County in the Munising area. Note the man in the front seat. He is holding a fawn in his lap!

A sleigh carrying children and adults slides down a roadway lined with massive snowbanks. Below, a team of horses pulls a snow grader along a village street.

There's room for both! Two modes of transportation—one of a passing era and another of the future — share a snow covered U.P road. This photo was taken in the Copper Country circa 1920s.

Chapter • 8 • Transportation

"Ah! Up ahead I see the shoreline."

Whoa! That didn't go as planned! The ice was evidently a little thin.

Chapter • 8 • Transportation

Experts recommend that ice be 8 to 12 inches thick for safe passage across a frozen lake by car or a small pickup.

In the days before U.P. roadways were cleared of snow, automobile tires were replaced with skis and cars were converted to sleds in the winter.

Chapter • 8 • Transportation

Electrified streetcars were the mass transit in major U.P. cities during the early portion of the 20th century. Streetcar service began in Marquette circa 1890.

During the great snowstorm of February 1922 streetcars became snowbound in Menominee. Farther north in Marquette, the Weather Bureau observer stated that "the streetcar sweeper is able to make the circuit of its tracks, but not the cars."

Chapter • 8 • Transportation

The cleared streetcar lines in Marquette enabled pedestrians to move north and south through town during and immediately after the 1922 storm. Sidewalks were said to be impassable, clogged with two to four feet of hard-packed snow.

Railroad transportation slowly developed across Upper Michigan. The first railroad was built between Lake Superior and the iron mines around Ishpeming in 1857. In 1864, a railroad was completed between Negaunee and Escanaba. The U.P. was finally connected to the rest of the United States when the Chicago and Northwestern Railroad completed extension of its track from Green Bay to Escanaba in 1872.

The expansion of the railroad into the interior opened the Menominee Range to iron mining near Iron Mountain in 1877. Seven years later the railroad reached the Gogebic Range at present-day Ironwood. On the east end, Sault Ste. Marie finally was connected to the rest of Upper Michigan and the country when the first railroad reached the city in January, 1888.

Keeping the rail lines open in winter across the Upper Michigan wilderness was often a challenge.

Chapter • 8 • Transportation

In the aftermath of the Storm of '38, a north-bound Chicago train stalled in a drift 30 feet high between Herman and Nestoria in Baraga County.

Even in the "Banana Belt" of the southern U.P. a train became snowbound at Ford River south of Escanaba.

Above railroad workers on a plow locomotive taking time for a photo op. Below, the Keweenaw Central Railroad plow circa 1900.

As locomotives became more powerful, the plows became larger and larger.

Chapter · 8 · Transportation

Today there is little chance a snowstorm could stall train travel!

Above, the Negaunee State Police post circa 1930-40s. Below is an early model State Police snowmobile. As you can see, it was not outfitted with the best safety features!

"As the snows accumulate on the ground, so do the contributions that the winter wonderland annually makes to the national economy mount."—David Ludlum

9
Shipwrecks

The main route for delivery of goods and exporting of resources out of Upper Michigan continued to be over the Great Lakes into the 20th century. The relatively small schooners and barges (compared to today's vessels) meant that there was a lot of ship traffic. Early settler and weather observer L. P. Crary counted as many as "sixty or seventy little craft in Marquette Harbor at one time." Still with all the traffic, Lake Superior sustained only 10 percent of the shipwrecks on the Great Lakes. This was because of the lighter traffic compared to the southern and eastern Great Lakes. At the same time, Lake Superior's isolation added to the danger.

A great deal of the lake's shoreline is rugged and rocky. In addition, much of its coast remained uninhabited through the early 20th century. If a boat grounded on the rocks, it could mean being stranded in the wilderness and dying of exposure. It is this feature that sets Lake Superior apart from the rest of the Great Lakes.

The schooners *Moonlight* and *Kent* stranded on the beach, east of Marquette in September 1895.

"A shipwreck. The wild waters roar and heave. The brave vessel is dashed all to pieces."
—*William Shakespeare*

On November 17, 1886 "the worst Northeaster ever known on this part of Lake Superior" set in at Marquette accompanied by blinding snow and sleet. "The wind seemed to increase in fury during the day." Vessels tied to the docks in the Lower Harbor had their lines snapped and were "compelled to go out and lie at anchor."

Chapter • 9 • Shipwrecks

The tugboat *Gillett* captained by John Frink had already saved a schooner from crashing into the breakwater when another vessel was spotted in distress. The schooner *Florida* was caught in the raging sea and her captain lost control of the vessel.

Frink eased the *Gillett* as close as possible to the distressed *Florida* while his crew assisted in rescuing the captain and crew of the doomed vessel. During the rescue, the captain's mate, hanging overboard clinging to the schooner, was crushed when a huge sea hurled the *Gillett* against the *Florida*. He later died of his injuries. The rest of the captain and crew leaped for their lives and were saved but their ship was lost.

The next day, some townsmen discovered two other vessels run aground. The *Robert Wallace* and her consort, *David Wallace* floundered about four miles east of Marquette. Attempts to shoot a line from shore to the 24 crewmen on board the vessels failed. It took nearly two days more before the nearly frozen sailors were saved by the Portage Life Saving service. The service, under the command of Captain Ocha, made a 110-mile train trip with boats and equipment in a blizzard and eventually made a successful rescue of every man on board the *Wallaces*.

Financial loss of the schooners totaled $300,000 including the 104,000 bushels of wheat the *Robert Wallace* carried. The vessels were refurbished only to have the *Robert Wallace* sink again near Two Harbors, Minnesota almost 16 years to the day of the Marquette wreck. In 2006, the remains of the *Wallace* were discovered in 235 feet of water.

The next year an unusually early snowstorm caused three more shipwrecks in the Marquette area. The storm was considered "almost the exact counterpart" to the gale of November 17-18, 1886. The steambarge *Hurlbut* limped into Marquette Harbor the second day of the storm and reported her consort *Plymouth* stranded at Presque Isle. Her crew was eventually rescued, but the *Plymouth* spent the winter as a frozen ghost ship encased in ice on the west end of Presque Isle.

Chapter · 9 · Shipwrecks

To the east of Marquette, two vessels met their demise on rocky Shot Point. The first schooner, *George Sherman* went up on the rocks when her captain wandered too close to shore in the blinding snowstorm. The crew was able to escape the doomed vessel in the ships yawl boat. The frozen, exhausted crew wandered in the woods for hours until they came upon the main railroad track into Marquette. Just after dark, an ore train came along and the crew hitched a ride into the city.

The crew of the other vessel, *Alva Bradley*, was not as fortunate. Their vessel went aground farther offshore and their lifeboat came loose and was lost. It took two days, but Captain Ocha and his brave crew again made the trip from Portage Canal and after much danger and misery plucked the 10-man crew off the *Bradley*. The wreck had a positive effect in that it led to the construction of Marquette's own Life Saving station which opened in 1891.

Chapter • 9 • Shipwrecks

The steamer *Chaffe* plied the waters of Lake Superior during the latter portion of the 19th century. Here it is pictured frozen in place with her crew posing for a photographer. This was likely one of many times she battled winter's worst.

In late December 1874, the *Chaffe* was reported fast in the ice as she attempted to leave Grand Island harbor at Munising.

A week later in early January 1875 the ship was still stuck in the ice about a mile offshore near Munising as the coldest weather of the icy winter of 1874-75 set in.

Chapter • 9 • Shipwrecks

The steamer *Kershaw* fell victim to a strong southwest gale east of Marquette in September 1895. She was towing two schooners pictured here, the *Moonlight* and the *Kent*. The captain of the *Kershaw* ordered the ships cut free just before his boat went aground on a rock reef east of Marquette. The Marquette Life Saving Service took the men off the stranded vessel in what was called "the greatest Lake Superior rescue of the 1890s." The schooners, pictured here, spent months stranded on the beach east of Marquette before they were towed free.

The shipping season of 1905 was declared "the most disastrous season in the history of shipping on the lakes." Pictured above left *Spencer,* above right *Edenborn.* Below *"Crescent City.* All went aground on the west end of Lake Superior in late November 1905.

Three major storms resulted in the loss of 199 men and 70 wrecked vessels. Total losses were placed at $7 million; around $180 million today.

Pictured on this page are two of the vessels wrecked by the last, and probably the worst of them all—the blizzard and gale of November 28-29, 1905.

During the height of the 1905 storm on the west end of the lake, the freighter *Mataafa* captained by Captain Richard Humble tried to make a run for safe harbor at Duluth in a furious easterly gale. As the captain tried to maneuver the ship into the canal, a huge following wave hit the ship and drove it to the lake bottom. The boat shot up and "T-boned" the north pier.

The *Mataafa* came to rest about 100 feet from the north pier with 12 crew members in the bow and 12 in the stern. The ship, essentially splitting in half, began flooding. Three of the men in the stern made it to the relative safety of the bow. Another man made three attempts to jump to the bow. Each time he was washed over by a wave and clutched the railing to keep from getting swept to his death in the icy water. He braced himself against the rail for a fourth attempt as a great swell rolled over him. After the soaking, he decided against another attempt and went back into the stern.

The next day the storm subsided enough for the Life-Saving Service to pull 15 crew members from the bow of the ship. The nine men in the stern perished. Some bodies were brought to shore encased in ice while some were never found.

The November 28-29, 1905 storm will forever be known as the "*Mataafa Storm*" on the west end of Lake Superior. While 9 men died when the ship grounded and split up, the worst storm tragedy occurred northeast of the Apostle Islands. The morning of the 28th, the freighter *Ira H. Owen* was spotted in distress by another vessel. Later, ships passed through wreckage from the vessel. The *Owen* and her crew of 19 were never seen again.

Chapter · 9 · Shipwrecks

Eight years later, the region was struck by another fierce November gale. From November 8-10, 1913 "Freshwater Fury" became the deadliest storm to ever strike the Great Lakes. Pictured here is one of its victims the *Turret Chief*.

The 273-foot *Turret Chief* and her crew were fortunate. The ship ran aground four miles east of Copper Harbor but those on board were saved and the ship was later salvaged.

Chapter • 9 • Shipwrecks

Farther east, just off Keweenaw Point, the *L.C. Waldo* rammed Gull Rock bow first in the predawn hours of November 8, 1913. The ship was already heavily damaged. Captain John Duddleston narrowly escaped being washed overboard when the pilot house was ripped off by a rogue wave. Then another wave took out the cabin housing the rest of the crew. Finally the captain and crew of 20 men and two women took refuge in the steel windlass house in the forward portion of the ship. They suffered with only a small fire and barely any food for two full days and parts of two more.

Another freighter spotted the *Waldo* and eventually the Life-Saving Services at Portage Canal and Eagle Harbor learned of the wreck. Brave crews from both locations battled bitter cold, stormy seas and equipment malfunction before reaching the vessel.

Chapter • 9 • Shipwrecks

Finally in the early morning light of November 11, 1913, the almost frozen survivors of the *L.C. Waldo* observed a grotesque, ghostly shape top a wave. As the apparition got closer the crew recognized the boat of the Portage Life-Saving station. They were saved! A portion of the crew boarded this boat while the rest of the crew was taken off the wreck by the Eagle Harbor Life-Savers.

To the southeast at Marquette, Captain Jimmy Owen was in a hurry. He had to get his boat, the ore carrier *Henry B. Smith* down to the Lower Lakes as quickly as possible. Owen, through circumstances out of his control, ran late all season. Rumor had it that he was given an ultimatum—deliver the last load of ore on time or stay on shore next season. In this photo Owen (on the far right) poses with a group of tourists visiting his ship.

Captain Owen made the unfortunate decision to leave Marquette Harbor late on Sunday, November 9, 1913, during a temporary lull in the storm. As his boat pulled away from the harbor, the blizzard came on again full force. Observers on shore watched the ship heave in the waves, and soon they lost sight of the *Smith* in a blinding snow squall. Captain Jimmy Owen and his crew of two dozen were never heard from again. They were among the more than 200 sailors lost in the Freshwater Fury of 1913.

Over the years, there were numerous attempts to locate the vessel to no avail. Finally 100 years later in the summer of 2013, a crew of shipwreck hunters out of Duluth found the ship in over 535 feet of water about 30 miles north of Marquette.

One of the most remarkable shipwrecks occurred during a November gale 13 years later in 1926. The steamer *City of Bangor* was upbound from Detroit on the way to Duluth. It's cargo was 248 brand new Chryslers. The ship rammed a reef rounding Keweenaw Point in a storm on the night of November 30, 1926.

The crew of the *Bangor* spent a night in the woods with inadequate clothing and provisions east of Copper Harbor. They were ultimately rescued by the Coast Guard.

As for the cars, 18 were swept off the deck and were never recovered. The other 230 vehicles were ultimately taken off the boat once the ice became thick enough to build a ramp off the ship.

A number of vehicles were housed in the ship's hold, but those on deck had to be carved out of thick ice and snow.

Chapter • 9 • Shipwrecks

Eventually all the vehicles were taken off the boat. In spring, the cars were driven south to Calumet. There they were loaded on a train to Detroit where they were inspected at the Chrysler factory, repaired and sold.

As for the *City of Bangor*, it remained on the rocks until World War II when it was cut up for scrap. Some of the vessel still remains where it went aground near Keweenaw Point.

The next year 1927, just east of where the *Bangor* went aground, the *Altadoc* met the same fate. Today the site is a scuba diving spot where the remains of the two ships are intermingled.

Chapter • 9 • Shipwrecks

On Armistice Day 1940 a tremendous storm fueled by bitter cold arctic air in the Rockies and warm, moist air off the Gulf of Mexico lashed the Upper Midwest. The storm track brought the worst conditions to Lake Michigan. Ferocious south gales blowing the length of the lake caused shipwrecks and the loss of 59 sailors.

A tidal surge drove water eight feet above normal into Little Bay De Noc. A fishing guide living in a cabin at the head of the bay in Rapid River was swept away cabin and all. The next day the top half of the house drifted back in but the body of the guide was never recovered.

During the height of the 1940 storm, the 416-foot steamer *Sinaloa* was blown off course when its engine failed. The boat rammed a rock ledge just off the Garden Peninsula. The captain and crew of 41 became stranded several hundred yards off shore. Garden Peninsula fishermen sprang into action and took off about half the crew. The Munising Coast Guard traveled overland to the wreck site and employed a breeches buoy to rescue the rest of the crew. The *Sinaloa* was eventually towed off the reef and repaired.

An early autumn gale grounded the 6000-ton ore carrier *Maryland* in September 1953 off Hiawatha Shores (now the beach adjacent to Lakewood Lane) just east of Marquette.

Marquette residents had a great photo opportunity in September 1953 as a Coast Guard helicopter battling strong northerly gales pulled 12 crew members off the grounded *Maryland*.

Chapter • 9 • Shipwrecks

The rest of the crew was taken off the *Maryland* with a breeches buoy—the last such rescue on the Great Lakes. The ship was later scrapped.

The 729-foot ore carrier *Edmund Fitzgerald* was christened and launched on the River Rouge in Detroit on June 7, 1958. It was the largest carrier on the lake at the time.

Chapter • 9 • Shipwrecks

The *Fitzgerald* was the pride of the Oglebay Norton Fleet. It set shipping records for years, probably in part because its captain, Ernest McSorley, had a reputation for always being in a hurry.

On November 9, 1975, the captain of the *Edmund Fitzgerald* took on a 26,000 ton load of iron ore at Superior, Wisconsin. Despite the forecast of a northeast gale, McSorley decided to take the usual Lake Carriers Association route right across the lake because it was the quickest route from Duluth to Sault Ste, Marie. That decision brought the *Fitzgerald* to exactly the wrong place at the wrong time the next evening.

McSorley tried to make a run for the relative safety of Whitefish Bay on the east side of the lake. Already damaged and listing, the *Fitzgerald* was hit with hurricane force wind gusts and waves exceeding 25 feet. The carrier went down with all 29 crew members about 17 miles northwest of Whitefish Point.

Chapter • 9 • Shipwrecks

Ships travel Lake Superior as long as the season will allow. In the old days before icebreakers, ships might become a prisoner of the ice. Pictured here is the Buoy Tender *U.S.S Marigold* trapped in the ice at Whitefish Point circa 1920.

Above, carriers at dock on a bitter day. Below, ships caught in late-season ice possibly in Whitefish Bay.

Chapter • 9 • Shipwrecks

The National Weather Service in Marquette issues forecasts for the U.S. waters of Lake Superior right through the winter. The forecast will often highlight a "Freezing Spray Warning." The vessels pictured here had rough trips, accumulating a tremendous amount of ice due to freezing spray.

Modern shipping on the lake still has a slow time when the Sault Locks close for repairs. In 2016, the locks closed January 15 and reopened on March 25. It was a warm winter and shipping was hardly impeded at all. In 2014 however, after one of the most severely cold winters on record, shipping was bogged down by ice well into spring. The story goes that a vessel left Duluth downbound for the locks with a Coast Guard icebreaker leading the way. A trip that would normally take about a day took two weeks due to thick ice!

10

The Greatest Snowstorm

I call it "The Storm Against which All Others are Measured." The "Storm of 1938" developed over east Texas on January 23 and headed northeastward with copious amounts of Gulf moisture. The low pressure system appeared to phase with energy dropping southeastward out of south-central Canada. This phasing caused a deepening and slowing of the forward movement of the low as it approached Upper Michigan from the southwest on January 24. The system headed through central Illinois into Lower Michigan in just the right location to give most of Upper Michigan heavy snow and gale-force winds. By the morning of January 25, an intense storm system was centered near Sault Ste. Marie.

Anyone who was old enough to remember has a story to tell about how they or a family member were affected by the crippling snowstorm. Fortunately, there are many photographs from the historic event and we showcase some in the following pages.

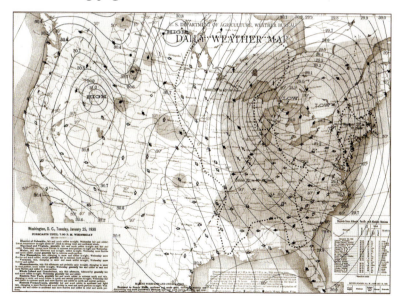

"Not even the 'old-timers' who like to spin yarns about 'the good old days' and the storms...
can tell a tale equal the one their children will be telling about this one."
—Duluth News-Tribune on the impact of the storm on the Gogebic Range

Sunburns to Snowstorms: Upper Michigan Weather in Pictures & Stories

This young man had quite a task clearing a sidewalk in downtown Marquette. The U.S. Weather Bureau in the city reported a total of 18 inches of snow in the storm with many areas getting much higher totals.

Chapter • 10 • The Greatest Snowstorm

Ironwood got buried under nearly three feet of snow. Munising received daily precipitation records of 1.75" and 1.15" respectively on January 25 and 26. Assuming a 10 to 1 ratio of snow to water would yield 29 inches of snow. The Copper Country was north of the heaviest snow. Below, Calumet received only 7 ½ inches, however, 50 mph winds blew the snow into huge drifts and the old-timers declared the storm "the worst of them all."

Above, drifts in the Copper Country reached 20 feet high. Below, the Eagle Harbor lighthouse was without electricity from Monday night, January 24 until Thursday evening. Freezing spray off Lake Superior coated the shore-facing side of the structure with eight inches of ice. The lighthouse keeper said the Storm of '38 was the worst storm in his 32 years of service.

Chapter • 10 • The Greatest Snowstorm

Children all over Upper Michigan enjoyed an extended vacation from school after the massive storm. Most played on the mountains of snow left by the storm, while this youngster preferred taking his sled through a doorway tunnel constructed in a Negaunee snowbank.

In rural areas, folks were cut off from the rest of the world until the snowplow came through. In some cases, it took days before roads were cleared. In town, snowbanks towered over people and automobiles.

Chapter • 10 • The Greatest Snowstorm

Scenes like this were played out all across Upper Michigan after the 36-hour Storm of '38.

The hotel Northland in Marquette became a concert hall as a troupe of singers from Finland was stranded for several days. They gave free performances in the lobby during their stay.

Chapter • 10 • The Greatest Snowstorm

Schools in Marquette and much of Upper Michigan were closed for up to a week. Below, in Marquette, Principal Willard Whitman peers around a mountain of snow left by the Storm of '38.

The snow fell initially with temperatures near to just above freezing. The sticky snow was then blown by gale-force winds and had the consistency of sand making clearing of the snow even more difficult.

Chapter • 10 • The Greatest Snowstorm

During the height of the storm, a fire broke out in the Masonic Temple in downtown Marquette. It was discovered and reported by paperboys in the early morning of Tuesday, January 25, 1938.

The fire destroyed four buildings on Washington Street with damage estimated at $400,000 ($7,000,000 in 2017). Heroic efforts by firemen contained the blaze but made a mess of downtown.

Chapter • 10 • The Greatest Snowstorm

The blaze was the worst fire in the city since the conflagration that consumed much of Marquette in 1868. One of the buildings destroyed was the Opera House that Marquette pioneer Peter White built.

In Negaunee, a group of men and children pose for a photographer on a mountain of snow on Iron Street. Below, pedestrians peer around snowbanks. In the 1930s when snow fell, it was plowed into piles alongside the street. The piles then remained until spring.

Chapter • 10 • The Greatest Snowstorm

Above residents of Negaunee enjoy a beautiful winter day a couple of days after the storm.

The iconic image below was turned into a postcard. At the height of the storm, authorities called crews off the roads until the storm abated.

A number of people told stories of how residents could not get out of their houses except by exiting through a second story window.

Chapter • 10 • The Greatest Snowstorm

These photos of Ishpeming in the aftermath of the Storm of '38 illustrate the quantity of snow that clogged the roads. Possibly a guest at the Mather Inn pictured below had to stay an extra night or two until his vehicle was dug out and the streets cleared.

More scenes of Ishpeming in the aftermath of the blizzard. After the storm, there was very little snow the rest of the season. In fact, the golf course in Marquette opened right around the first day of spring on March 22.

Chapter • 10 • The Greatest Snowstorm

Above, a wing plow does battle against the drifts. There was less snow removal equipment in 1938 than today and the plows were much less powerful. Below, another view of Ishpeming after the Storm of '38; a storm that lives on as one of *the* major weather events in Upper Michigan history.

Above, Iron Street in Negaunee is reduced to a pedestrian walkway. Did the ladies on the right without their coats just make an appearance for this photo opportunity? Below, workers at one of the city yards in Negaunee take a break.

11

Winter's Beauty

The Great Lakes contain 20 percent of the world's fresh water; Lake Superior holds as much as the other Great Lakes combined. These vast bodies of fresh water are whipped into a frenzy by gales in the fall and winter. The result on shore is frozen, almost surreal beauty. All the following photographs were taken by Jack Deo unless otherwise noted.

A Snowshoe Party, Sault Ste. Marie, Mich.

"I've lived in good climate and it bores the hell out of me. I like weather rather than climate."
— *John Steinbeck*

Three images of the same cottage on Middle Island Point near Marquette: Top, in the aftermath of the Storm of '38; bottom left a photo taken by Jack in the 1970s and right, the authors posing in front of the structure in early March 2017.

Chapter • 11 • Winter's Beauty

Two views of the same cabin on Middle Island Point encased in ice circa 1970s.

Above, Middle Island Point cabin encased in ice. Below Cindy Deo in Wonderland, Middle Island Point circa 1970s.

Chapter • 11 • Winter's Beauty

Above, "Storm Windows"; Below, another ice-encased cabin on Middle Island Point circa 1970s.

Two more seasonal camps that fell victim to the furious waves off Lake Superior during the Storm of '38.

Chapter • 11 • Winter's Beauty

Two more views of iced up seasonal camps at Middle Island Point near Marquette after the Storm of '38.

A winter view of the St. Joseph lighthouse on Lake Michigan.

Chapter • 11 • Winter's Beauty

Another view of the St. Joseph lighthouse circa 1920s.

Above, two views of a birdhouse bent over from the accumulation of ice. Obviously the birds consider this a seasonal dwelling, too! Below, the old Marquette lighthouse.

"What good is the warmth of summer, without the cold of winter to give it sweetness."
—*John Steinbeck*

12

Fashion of the Season

Residents of Upper Michigan battle winter's worst with pride and "Sisu" (a Finnish word meaning strength of will, determination and perseverance). Back in the late 19th century and beyond, they also did it in style. The following pages give examples of Yooper winter wear through the years.

Child's Art Gallery, Ishpeming circa early 1890s

"Fashion is a language that creates itself in clothes to interpret reality."
— *Karl Lagerfeld*

Sunburns to Snowstorms: Upper Michigan Weather in Pictures & Stories

Above left, snowy conversations, circa 1918 in Menominee. Top right, Negaunee snowball fight early 1890s. The gentleman appears to have been on the losing end of the fight! Below, ladies in the Munising area brandishing ice swords.

Chapter • 12 • Fashion of the Season

Above, Marquette Snowshoe Club circa 1880s. The second man standing on the left is John M. Longyear, prominent businessman and land owner. Below, even babies and small children sported their unique fashions circa 1900.

Above, more images taken by B.F. Childs circa 1890s. Below the Kennedy sisters and friends, Marquette circa 1890s.

Chapter • 12 • Fashion of the Season

The dapper gentlemen above modeled the latest fashion in winter coats circa 1890s. Below on left, children pose in their winter's best Mongolian lamb's fur clothing in Ishpeming circa 1890s, On the right, the child modeling winter wear is Pearl Burrows (Yelland) grandmother of this book's artist. All photographs taken in the early 1900s at the Child's Art Gallery.

Ready to hit the slopes, these men were members of the Nordeen Ski Club, Ishpeming circa 1880s.

Chapter • 12 • Fashion of the Season

The children's chapter of the Marquette Snowshoe Club displaying a northern Scandinavian influence circa 1890s

Above, the Marquette Winter Carnival "Giant Ski" of the early 1940s. The young lady in line second from the right is Anita Meyland who initiated Marquette's premiere summer event "Art on the Rocks." Below, the gents from "Marketty" Camp near Negaunee circa 1890s

Chapter • 12 • Fashion of the Season

Winter Scene in Government Park, Saulte Ste. Marie. Below left, Ishpeming ski jumper, Leonard Bietala, second oldest of five brothers known as the "Flying Bietalas", proudly poses with his skis. Right, these ladies hats were obviously designed for looks, not for protection from winter's worst. Their fur capes were made of Persian Lamb.

Sunburns to Snowstorms: Upper Michigan Weather in Pictures & Stories

So long folks! Above, teenagers sliding along a snow-covered road after the monster storm of February 1922. Below, 95 years later the authors have much less snow to deal with at Marquette's Presque Isle.